this bucket list belongs to

_____

_____

"never give up because great things take time"

OUR BUCKET LIST

WE WANT TO DO THIS BECAUSE

_____
_____
_____
_____

OUR MEMORIES AND THOUGHTS

_____
_____
_____
_____
_____
_____
_____
_____

COMPLETION DATE

_____

WOULD WE DO IT AGAIN?　　YES ☐　　NO ☐

OUR BUCKET LIST

WE WANT TO DO THIS BECAUSE

_____
_____
_____
_____

OUR MEMORIES AND THOUGHTS

_____
_____
_____
_____
_____
_____
_____
_____

COMPLETION DATE

_____

WOULD WE DO IT AGAIN?   YES ☐   NO ☐

OUR BUCKET LIST

WE WANT TO DO THIS BECAUSE

_____
_____
_____
_____

OUR MEMORIES AND THOUGHTS

_____
_____
_____
_____
_____
_____
_____
_____

COMPLETION DATE

_____

WOULD WE DO IT AGAIN?   YES ☐   NO ☐

OUR BUCKET LIST

WE WANT TO DO THIS BECAUSE

_____
_____
_____
_____

OUR MEMORIES AND THOUGHTS

_____
_____
_____
_____
_____
_____
_____
_____

COMPLETION DATE

_____

WOULD WE DO IT AGAIN?　　YES ☐　　NO ☐

OUR BUCKET LIST

WE WANT TO DO THIS BECAUSE

_____
_____
_____
_____

OUR MEMORIES AND THOUGHTS

_____
_____
_____
_____
_____
_____
_____
_____

COMPLETION DATE

_____

WOULD WE DO IT AGAIN? YES ☐ NO ☐

OUR BUCKET LIST

WE WANT TO DO THIS BECAUSE

_____
_____
_____
_____

OUR MEMORIES AND THOUGHTS

_____
_____
_____
_____
_____
_____
_____
_____

COMPLETION DATE

_____

WOULD WE DO IT AGAIN?　　YES ☐　　NO ☐

OUR BUCKET LIST

WE WANT TO DO THIS BECAUSE

_____
_____
_____
_____

OUR MEMORIES AND THOUGHTS

_____
_____
_____
_____
_____
_____
_____
_____

COMPLETION DATE

_____

WOULD WE DO IT AGAIN?   YES ☐   NO ☐

OUR BUCKET LIST

WE WANT TO DO THIS BECAUSE

_____
_____
_____
_____
_____

OUR MEMORIES AND THOUGHTS

_____
_____
_____
_____
_____
_____
_____
_____
_____

COMPLETION DATE

_____

WOULD WE DO IT AGAIN?   YES ☐   NO ☐

OUR BUCKET LIST

WE WANT TO DO THIS BECAUSE

_____
_____
_____
_____

OUR MEMORIES AND THOUGHTS

_____
_____
_____
_____
_____
_____
_____
_____

COMPLETION DATE

_____

WOULD WE DO IT AGAIN?   YES ☐   NO ☐

OUR BUCKET LIST

WE WANT TO DO THIS BECAUSE

_____
_____
_____
_____

OUR MEMORIES AND THOUGHTS

_____
_____
_____
_____
_____
_____
_____
_____

COMPLETION DATE

_____

WOULD WE DO IT AGAIN?   YES ☐   NO ☐

OUR BUCKET LIST

WE WANT TO DO THIS BECAUSE

_____
_____
_____
_____

OUR MEMORIES AND THOUGHTS

_____
_____
_____
_____
_____
_____
_____
_____
_____

COMPLETION DATE

_____

WOULD WE DO IT AGAIN?   YES ☐   NO ☐

OUR BUCKET LIST

WE WANT TO DO THIS BECAUSE

_____
_____
_____
_____

OUR MEMORIES AND THOUGHTS

_____
_____
_____
_____
_____
_____
_____
_____

COMPLETION DATE

_____

WOULD WE DO IT AGAIN? YES ☐ NO ☐

OUR BUCKET LIST

WE WANT TO DO THIS BECAUSE

_____
_____
_____

OUR MEMORIES AND THOUGHTS

_____
_____
_____
_____
_____
_____
_____
_____

COMPLETION DATE

_____

WOULD WE DO IT AGAIN?   YES ☐   NO ☐

OUR BUCKET LIST

WE WANT TO DO THIS BECAUSE

_____
_____
_____
_____

OUR MEMORIES AND THOUGHTS

_____
_____
_____
_____
_____
_____
_____
_____

COMPLETION DATE

_____

WOULD WE DO IT AGAIN?   YES ☐   NO ☐

OUR BUCKET LIST

WE WANT TO DO THIS BECAUSE

_____
_____
_____
_____

OUR MEMORIES AND THOUGHTS

_____
_____
_____
_____
_____
_____
_____
_____

COMPLETION DATE

_____

WOULD WE DO IT AGAIN?   YES ☐   NO ☐

OUR BUCKET LIST

WE WANT TO DO THIS BECAUSE

_____
_____
_____
_____

OUR MEMORIES AND THOUGHTS

_____
_____
_____
_____
_____
_____
_____
_____

COMPLETION DATE

_____

WOULD WE DO IT AGAIN?   YES ☐   NO ☐

OUR BUCKET LIST

WE WANT TO DO THIS BECAUSE

_____
_____
_____
_____

OUR MEMORIES AND THOUGHTS

_____
_____
_____
_____
_____
_____
_____
_____

COMPLETION DATE

_____

WOULD WE DO IT AGAIN?   YES ☐   NO ☐

OUR BUCKET LIST

WE WANT TO DO THIS BECAUSE

_____
_____
_____
_____

OUR MEMORIES AND THOUGHTS

_____
_____
_____
_____
_____
_____
_____
_____

COMPLETION DATE

_____

WOULD WE DO IT AGAIN?   YES ☐   NO ☐

OUR BUCKET LIST

WE WANT TO DO THIS BECAUSE

_____
_____
_____
_____

OUR MEMORIES AND THOUGHTS

_____
_____
_____
_____
_____
_____
_____
_____

COMPLETION DATE

_____

WOULD WE DO IT AGAIN?   YES ☐   NO ☐

OUR BUCKET LIST

WE WANT TO DO THIS BECAUSE

_____
_____
_____
_____

OUR MEMORIES AND THOUGHTS

_____
_____
_____
_____
_____
_____
_____
_____

COMPLETION DATE

_____

WOULD WE DO IT AGAIN?   YES ☐   NO ☐

OUR BUCKET LIST

WE WANT TO DO THIS BECAUSE

_____
_____
_____
_____

OUR MEMORIES AND THOUGHTS

_____
_____
_____
_____
_____
_____
_____
_____

COMPLETION DATE

_____

WOULD WE DO IT AGAIN?   YES ☐   NO ☐

OUR BUCKET LIST

WE WANT TO DO THIS BECAUSE

_____
_____
_____
_____

OUR MEMORIES AND THOUGHTS

_____
_____
_____
_____
_____
_____
_____
_____

COMPLETION DATE

_____

WOULD WE DO IT AGAIN?　　YES ☐　　NO ☐

OUR BUCKET LIST

WE WANT TO DO THIS BECAUSE

_____
_____
_____
_____

OUR MEMORIES AND THOUGHTS

_____
_____
_____
_____
_____
_____
_____
_____

COMPLETION DATE

_____

WOULD WE DO IT AGAIN?   YES ☐   NO ☐

OUR BUCKET LIST

WE WANT TO DO THIS BECAUSE

_____
_____
_____
_____
_____

OUR MEMORIES AND THOUGHTS

_____
_____
_____
_____
_____
_____
_____
_____
_____

COMPLETION DATE

_____

WOULD WE DO IT AGAIN?　　YES ☐　　NO ☐

OUR BUCKET LIST

WE WANT TO DO THIS BECAUSE

_____
_____
_____
_____

OUR MEMORIES AND THOUGHTS

_____
_____
_____
_____
_____
_____
_____
_____

COMPLETION DATE

_____

WOULD WE DO IT AGAIN?   YES ☐   NO ☐

OUR BUCKET LIST

WE WANT TO DO THIS BECAUSE

_____
_____
_____
_____

OUR MEMORIES AND THOUGHTS

_____
_____
_____
_____
_____
_____
_____
_____

COMPLETION DATE

_____

WOULD WE DO IT AGAIN?   YES ☐   NO ☐

OUR BUCKET LIST

WE WANT TO DO THIS BECAUSE

_____
_____
_____
_____

OUR MEMORIES AND THOUGHTS

_____
_____
_____
_____
_____
_____
_____
_____

COMPLETION DATE

_____

WOULD WE DO IT AGAIN?   YES ☐   NO ☐

OUR BUCKET LIST

WE WANT TO DO THIS BECAUSE

_____
_____
_____
_____

OUR MEMORIES AND THOUGHTS

_____
_____
_____
_____
_____
_____
_____
_____

COMPLETION DATE

_____

WOULD WE DO IT AGAIN?   YES ☐   NO ☐

OUR BUCKET LIST

WE WANT TO DO THIS BECAUSE

_____
_____
_____
_____

OUR MEMORIES AND THOUGHTS

_____
_____
_____
_____
_____
_____
_____
_____

COMPLETION DATE

_____

WOULD WE DO IT AGAIN?   YES ☐   NO ☐

OUR BUCKET LIST

WE WANT TO DO THIS BECAUSE

_____
_____
_____
_____
_____

OUR MEMORIES AND THOUGHTS

_____
_____
_____
_____
_____
_____
_____
_____

COMPLETION DATE

_____

WOULD WE DO IT AGAIN?   YES ☐   NO ☐

OUR BUCKET LIST

WE WANT TO DO THIS BECAUSE

_____
_____
_____
_____

OUR MEMORIES AND THOUGHTS

_____
_____
_____
_____
_____
_____
_____

COMPLETION DATE

_____

WOULD WE DO IT AGAIN?   YES ☐   NO ☐

OUR BUCKET LIST

WE WANT TO DO THIS BECAUSE

_____
_____
_____
_____

OUR MEMORIES AND THOUGHTS

_____
_____
_____
_____
_____
_____
_____
_____

COMPLETION DATE

_____

WOULD WE DO IT AGAIN?   YES ☐   NO ☐

OUR BUCKET LIST

WE WANT TO DO THIS BECAUSE

_____
_____
_____
_____

OUR MEMORIES AND THOUGHTS

_____
_____
_____
_____
_____
_____
_____
_____

COMPLETION DATE

_____

WOULD WE DO IT AGAIN?   YES ☐   NO ☐

OUR BUCKET LIST

WE WANT TO DO THIS BECAUSE

_____
_____
_____
_____

OUR MEMORIES AND THOUGHTS

_____
_____
_____
_____
_____
_____
_____
_____

COMPLETION DATE

_____

WOULD WE DO IT AGAIN?   YES ☐   NO ☐

OUR BUCKET LIST

WE WANT TO DO THIS BECAUSE

_____
_____
_____
_____

OUR MEMORIES AND THOUGHTS

_____
_____
_____
_____
_____
_____
_____
_____

COMPLETION DATE

_____

WOULD WE DO IT AGAIN?   YES ☐   NO ☐

OUR BUCKET LIST

WE WANT TO DO THIS BECAUSE

_____
_____
_____
_____

OUR MEMORIES AND THOUGHTS

_____
_____
_____
_____
_____
_____
_____
_____

COMPLETION DATE

_____

WOULD WE DO IT AGAIN?   YES ☐   NO ☐

OUR BUCKET LIST

WE WANT TO DO THIS BECAUSE

_____
_____
_____

OUR MEMORIES AND THOUGHTS

_____
_____
_____
_____
_____
_____
_____

COMPLETION DATE

_____

WOULD WE DO IT AGAIN?   YES ☐   NO ☐

OUR BUCKET LIST

WE WANT TO DO THIS BECAUSE

_____
_____
_____
_____
_____

OUR MEMORIES AND THOUGHTS

_____
_____
_____
_____
_____
_____
_____
_____
_____
_____

COMPLETION DATE

_____

WOULD WE DO IT AGAIN?   YES ☐   NO ☐

OUR BUCKET LIST

WE WANT TO DO THIS BECAUSE

_____
_____
_____
_____

OUR MEMORIES AND THOUGHTS

_____
_____
_____
_____
_____
_____
_____
_____

COMPLETION DATE

_____

WOULD WE DO IT AGAIN?   YES ☐   NO ☐

OUR BUCKET LIST

WE WANT TO DO THIS BECAUSE

_____
_____
_____
_____

OUR MEMORIES AND THOUGHTS

_____
_____
_____
_____
_____
_____
_____
_____

COMPLETION DATE

_____

WOULD WE DO IT AGAIN?   YES ☐   NO ☐

OUR BUCKET LIST

WE WANT TO DO THIS BECAUSE

_____
_____
_____
_____

OUR MEMORIES AND THOUGHTS

_____
_____
_____
_____
_____
_____
_____
_____

COMPLETION DATE

_____

WOULD WE DO IT AGAIN?   YES ☐   NO ☐

OUR BUCKET LIST

WE WANT TO DO THIS BECAUSE

_____
_____
_____
_____

OUR MEMORIES AND THOUGHTS

_____
_____
_____
_____
_____
_____
_____
_____

COMPLETION DATE

_____

WOULD WE DO IT AGAIN?   YES ☐   NO ☐

OUR BUCKET LIST

WE WANT TO DO THIS BECAUSE

_____
_____
_____
_____

OUR MEMORIES AND THOUGHTS

_____
_____
_____
_____
_____
_____
_____
_____

COMPLETION DATE

_____

WOULD WE DO IT AGAIN?   YES ☐   NO ☐

OUR BUCKET LIST

WE WANT TO DO THIS BECAUSE

_____
_____
_____
_____

OUR MEMORIES AND THOUGHTS

_____
_____
_____
_____
_____
_____
_____
_____

COMPLETION DATE

_____

WOULD WE DO IT AGAIN?   YES ☐   NO ☐

OUR BUCKET LIST

WE WANT TO DO THIS BECAUSE

_____
_____
_____
_____

OUR MEMORIES AND THOUGHTS

_____
_____
_____
_____
_____
_____
_____
_____

COMPLETION DATE

_____

WOULD WE DO IT AGAIN?   YES ☐   NO ☐

OUR BUCKET LIST

WE WANT TO DO THIS BECAUSE

_____
_____
_____
_____

OUR MEMORIES AND THOUGHTS

_____
_____
_____
_____
_____
_____
_____
_____
_____

COMPLETION DATE

_____

WOULD WE DO IT AGAIN?   YES ☐   NO ☐

OUR BUCKET LIST

WE WANT TO DO THIS BECAUSE

_____
_____
_____
_____

OUR MEMORIES AND THOUGHTS

_____
_____
_____
_____
_____
_____
_____
_____

COMPLETION DATE

_____

WOULD WE DO IT AGAIN?   YES ☐   NO ☐

OUR BUCKET LIST

WE WANT TO DO THIS BECAUSE

_____
_____
_____
_____
_____

OUR MEMORIES AND THOUGHTS

_____
_____
_____
_____
_____
_____
_____
_____

COMPLETION DATE

_____

WOULD WE DO IT AGAIN?   YES ☐   NO ☐

OUR BUCKET LIST

WE WANT TO DO THIS BECAUSE

_____
_____
_____
_____

OUR MEMORIES AND THOUGHTS

_____
_____
_____
_____
_____
_____
_____

COMPLETION DATE

_____

WOULD WE DO IT AGAIN? YES ☐ NO ☐

OUR BUCKET LIST

WE WANT TO DO THIS BECAUSE

_____
_____
_____
_____

OUR MEMORIES AND THOUGHTS

_____
_____
_____
_____
_____
_____
_____
_____

COMPLETION DATE

_____

WOULD WE DO IT AGAIN?   YES ☐   NO ☐

OUR BUCKET LIST

WE WANT TO DO THIS BECAUSE

_____
_____
_____
_____

OUR MEMORIES AND THOUGHTS

_____
_____
_____
_____
_____
_____
_____
_____
_____

COMPLETION DATE

_____

WOULD WE DO IT AGAIN?   YES ☐   NO ☐

OUR BUCKET LIST

WE WANT TO DO THIS BECAUSE

_____
_____
_____
_____
_____

OUR MEMORIES AND THOUGHTS

_____
_____
_____
_____
_____
_____
_____
_____
_____

COMPLETION DATE

_____

WOULD WE DO IT AGAIN?　　YES ☐　　NO ☐

OUR BUCKET LIST

WE WANT TO DO THIS BECAUSE

_____
_____
_____
_____

OUR MEMORIES AND THOUGHTS

_____
_____
_____
_____
_____
_____
_____
_____

COMPLETION DATE

_____

WOULD WE DO IT AGAIN?   YES ☐   NO ☐

OUR BUCKET LIST

WE WANT TO DO THIS BECAUSE

_____
_____
_____
_____

OUR MEMORIES AND THOUGHTS

_____
_____
_____
_____
_____
_____
_____
_____

COMPLETION DATE

_____

WOULD WE DO IT AGAIN? YES ☐ NO ☐

OUR BUCKET LIST

WE WANT TO DO THIS BECAUSE

_____
_____
_____
_____

OUR MEMORIES AND THOUGHTS

_____
_____
_____
_____
_____
_____
_____
_____

COMPLETION DATE

_____

WOULD WE DO IT AGAIN? YES ☐   NO ☐

OUR BUCKET LIST

WE WANT TO DO THIS BECAUSE

_____
_____
_____
_____

OUR MEMORIES AND THOUGHTS

_____
_____
_____
_____
_____
_____
_____
_____

COMPLETION DATE

_____

WOULD WE DO IT AGAIN?   YES ☐   NO ☐

OUR BUCKET LIST

WE WANT TO DO THIS BECAUSE

_____
_____
_____
_____

OUR MEMORIES AND THOUGHTS

_____
_____
_____
_____
_____
_____
_____
_____

COMPLETION DATE

_____

WOULD WE DO IT AGAIN?   YES ☐   NO ☐

OUR BUCKET LIST

WE WANT TO DO THIS BECAUSE

_____
_____
_____
_____

OUR MEMORIES AND THOUGHTS

_____
_____
_____
_____
_____
_____
_____
_____

COMPLETION DATE

_____

WOULD WE DO IT AGAIN?   YES ☐   NO ☐

OUR BUCKET LIST

WE WANT TO DO THIS BECAUSE

_____
_____
_____
_____

OUR MEMORIES AND THOUGHTS

_____
_____
_____
_____
_____
_____
_____
_____

COMPLETION DATE

_____

WOULD WE DO IT AGAIN?   YES ☐   NO ☐

OUR BUCKET LIST

WE WANT TO DO THIS BECAUSE

_____
_____
_____
_____

OUR MEMORIES AND THOUGHTS

_____
_____
_____
_____
_____
_____
_____
_____

COMPLETION DATE

_____

WOULD WE DO IT AGAIN? YES ☐ NO ☐

OUR BUCKET LIST

WE WANT TO DO THIS BECAUSE

_____
_____
_____
_____

OUR MEMORIES AND THOUGHTS

_____
_____
_____
_____
_____
_____
_____
_____

COMPLETION DATE

_____

WOULD WE DO IT AGAIN?   YES ☐   NO ☐

OUR BUCKET LIST

WE WANT TO DO THIS BECAUSE

_____
_____
_____
_____

OUR MEMORIES AND THOUGHTS

_____
_____
_____
_____
_____
_____
_____
_____

COMPLETION DATE

_____

WOULD WE DO IT AGAIN?   YES ☐   NO ☐

OUR BUCKET LIST

WE WANT TO DO THIS BECAUSE

_____
_____
_____
_____

OUR MEMORIES AND THOUGHTS

_____
_____
_____
_____
_____
_____
_____
_____

COMPLETION DATE

_____

WOULD WE DO IT AGAIN?   YES ☐   NO ☐

OUR BUCKET LIST

WE WANT TO DO THIS BECAUSE

_____
_____
_____
_____

OUR MEMORIES AND THOUGHTS

_____
_____
_____
_____
_____
_____
_____
_____

COMPLETION DATE

_____

WOULD WE DO IT AGAIN?   YES ☐   NO ☐

OUR BUCKET LIST

WE WANT TO DO THIS BECAUSE

_____
_____
_____
_____

OUR MEMORIES AND THOUGHTS

_____
_____
_____
_____
_____
_____
_____
_____

COMPLETION DATE

_____

WOULD WE DO IT AGAIN?   YES ☐   NO ☐

OUR BUCKET LIST

WE WANT TO DO THIS BECAUSE

_____
_____
_____
_____
_____

OUR MEMORIES AND THOUGHTS

_____
_____
_____
_____
_____
_____
_____
_____
_____

COMPLETION DATE

_____

WOULD WE DO IT AGAIN?   YES ☐   NO ☐

OUR BUCKET LIST

WE WANT TO DO THIS BECAUSE

_____
_____
_____
_____

OUR MEMORIES AND THOUGHTS

_____
_____
_____
_____
_____
_____
_____
_____

COMPLETION DATE

_____

WOULD WE DO IT AGAIN?   YES ☐   NO ☐

OUR BUCKET LIST

WE WANT TO DO THIS BECAUSE

_____
_____
_____
_____
_____

OUR MEMORIES AND THOUGHTS

_____
_____
_____
_____
_____
_____
_____
_____
_____

COMPLETION DATE

_____

WOULD WE DO IT AGAIN?   YES ☐   NO ☐

OUR BUCKET LIST

WE WANT TO DO THIS BECAUSE

_____
_____
_____
_____

OUR MEMORIES AND THOUGHTS

_____
_____
_____
_____
_____
_____
_____
_____

COMPLETION DATE

_____

WOULD WE DO IT AGAIN?   YES ☐   NO ☐

OUR BUCKET LIST

WE WANT TO DO THIS BECAUSE

_____
_____
_____
_____

OUR MEMORIES AND THOUGHTS

_____
_____
_____
_____
_____
_____
_____
_____

COMPLETION DATE

_____

WOULD WE DO IT AGAIN? YES ☐   NO ☐

OUR BUCKET LIST

WE WANT TO DO THIS BECAUSE

_____
_____
_____
_____

OUR MEMORIES AND THOUGHTS

_____
_____
_____
_____
_____
_____
_____
_____

COMPLETION DATE

_____

WOULD WE DO IT AGAIN?   YES ☐   NO ☐

OUR BUCKET LIST

WE WANT TO DO THIS BECAUSE

_____
_____
_____
_____

OUR MEMORIES AND THOUGHTS

_____
_____
_____
_____
_____
_____
_____
_____

COMPLETION DATE

_____

WOULD WE DO IT AGAIN?   YES ☐   NO ☐

OUR BUCKET LIST

WE WANT TO DO THIS BECAUSE

_____
_____
_____
_____

OUR MEMORIES AND THOUGHTS

_____
_____
_____
_____
_____
_____
_____
_____

COMPLETION DATE

_____

WOULD WE DO IT AGAIN?   YES ☐   NO ☐

OUR BUCKET LIST

WE WANT TO DO THIS BECAUSE

_____
_____
_____
_____
_____

OUR MEMORIES AND THOUGHTS

_____
_____
_____
_____
_____
_____
_____
_____
_____
_____

COMPLETION DATE

_____

WOULD WE DO IT AGAIN? YES ☐   NO ☐

OUR BUCKET LIST

WE WANT TO DO THIS BECAUSE

_____
_____
_____
_____

OUR MEMORIES AND THOUGHTS

_____
_____
_____
_____
_____
_____
_____
_____

COMPLETION DATE

_____

WOULD WE DO IT AGAIN?   YES ☐   NO ☐

OUR BUCKET LIST

WE WANT TO DO THIS BECAUSE

_____
_____
_____
_____

OUR MEMORIES AND THOUGHTS

_____
_____
_____
_____
_____
_____
_____
_____
_____

COMPLETION DATE

_____

WOULD WE DO IT AGAIN?   YES ☐   NO ☐

OUR BUCKET LIST

WE WANT TO DO THIS BECAUSE

_____
_____
_____
_____

OUR MEMORIES AND THOUGHTS

_____
_____
_____
_____
_____
_____
_____
_____

COMPLETION DATE

_____

WOULD WE DO IT AGAIN?   YES ☐   NO ☐

OUR BUCKET LIST

WE WANT TO DO THIS BECAUSE

_____
_____
_____
_____

OUR MEMORIES AND THOUGHTS

_____
_____
_____
_____
_____
_____
_____
_____

COMPLETION DATE

_____

WOULD WE DO IT AGAIN?   YES ☐   NO ☐

OUR BUCKET LIST

WE WANT TO DO THIS BECAUSE

_____
_____
_____
_____

OUR MEMORIES AND THOUGHTS

_____
_____
_____
_____
_____
_____
_____

COMPLETION DATE

_____

WOULD WE DO IT AGAIN?   YES ☐   NO ☐

OUR BUCKET LIST

WE WANT TO DO THIS BECAUSE

_____
_____
_____
_____

OUR MEMORIES AND THOUGHTS

_____
_____
_____
_____
_____
_____
_____
_____

COMPLETION DATE

_____

WOULD WE DO IT AGAIN?   YES ☐   NO ☐

OUR BUCKET LIST

WE WANT TO DO THIS BECAUSE

_____
_____
_____
_____

OUR MEMORIES AND THOUGHTS

_____
_____
_____
_____
_____
_____
_____
_____

COMPLETION DATE

_____

WOULD WE DO IT AGAIN?   YES ☐   NO ☐

OUR BUCKET LIST

WE WANT TO DO THIS BECAUSE

_____
_____
_____
_____

OUR MEMORIES AND THOUGHTS

_____
_____
_____
_____
_____
_____
_____
_____
_____

COMPLETION DATE

_____

WOULD WE DO IT AGAIN?   YES ☐   NO ☐

OUR BUCKET LIST

WE WANT TO DO THIS BECAUSE

_____
_____
_____
_____

OUR MEMORIES AND THOUGHTS

_____
_____
_____
_____
_____
_____
_____
_____

COMPLETION DATE

_____

WOULD WE DO IT AGAIN?   YES ☐   NO ☐

OUR BUCKET LIST

WE WANT TO DO THIS BECAUSE

_____
_____
_____
_____

OUR MEMORIES AND THOUGHTS

_____
_____
_____
_____
_____
_____
_____
_____

COMPLETION DATE

_____

WOULD WE DO IT AGAIN?   YES ☐   NO ☐

OUR BUCKET LIST

WE WANT TO DO THIS BECAUSE

_____
_____
_____
_____

OUR MEMORIES AND THOUGHTS

_____
_____
_____
_____
_____
_____
_____
_____

COMPLETION DATE

_____

WOULD WE DO IT AGAIN?   YES ☐   NO ☐

OUR BUCKET LIST

WE WANT TO DO THIS BECAUSE

_____
_____
_____
_____
_____

OUR MEMORIES AND THOUGHTS

_____
_____
_____
_____
_____
_____
_____
_____
_____
_____

COMPLETION DATE

_____

WOULD WE DO IT AGAIN?   YES ☐   NO ☐

OUR BUCKET LIST

WE WANT TO DO THIS BECAUSE

_____
_____
_____
_____

OUR MEMORIES AND THOUGHTS

_____
_____
_____
_____
_____
_____
_____
_____

COMPLETION DATE

_____

WOULD WE DO IT AGAIN?   YES ☐   NO ☐

OUR BUCKET LIST

WE WANT TO DO THIS BECAUSE

_____
_____
_____
_____

OUR MEMORIES AND THOUGHTS

_____
_____
_____
_____
_____
_____
_____
_____

COMPLETION DATE

_____

WOULD WE DO IT AGAIN?　　YES ☐　　NO ☐

OUR BUCKET LIST

WE WANT TO DO THIS BECAUSE

_____
_____
_____
_____

OUR MEMORIES AND THOUGHTS

_____
_____
_____
_____
_____
_____
_____
_____

COMPLETION DATE

_____

WOULD WE DO IT AGAIN? YES ☐ NO ☐

OUR BUCKET LIST

WE WANT TO DO THIS BECAUSE

_____
_____
_____
_____

OUR MEMORIES AND THOUGHTS

_____
_____
_____
_____
_____
_____
_____

COMPLETION DATE

_____

WOULD WE DO IT AGAIN?   YES ☐   NO ☐

OUR BUCKET LIST

WE WANT TO DO THIS BECAUSE

_____
_____
_____
_____

OUR MEMORIES AND THOUGHTS

_____
_____
_____
_____
_____
_____
_____
_____

COMPLETION DATE

_____

WOULD WE DO IT AGAIN?   YES ☐   NO ☐

OUR BUCKET LIST

WE WANT TO DO THIS BECAUSE

_____
_____
_____
_____
_____

OUR MEMORIES AND THOUGHTS

_____
_____
_____
_____
_____
_____
_____
_____
_____
_____

COMPLETION DATE

_____

WOULD WE DO IT AGAIN?   YES ☐   NO ☐

OUR BUCKET LIST

WE WANT TO DO THIS BECAUSE

_____
_____
_____
_____

OUR MEMORIES AND THOUGHTS

_____
_____
_____
_____
_____
_____
_____
_____

COMPLETION DATE

_____

WOULD WE DO IT AGAIN?   YES ☐   NO ☐

OUR BUCKET LIST

WE WANT TO DO THIS BECAUSE

_____
_____
_____
_____

OUR MEMORIES AND THOUGHTS

_____
_____
_____
_____
_____
_____
_____
_____

COMPLETION DATE

_____

WOULD WE DO IT AGAIN?   YES ☐   NO ☐

OUR BUCKET LIST

WE WANT TO DO THIS BECAUSE

_____
_____
_____
_____

OUR MEMORIES AND THOUGHTS

_____
_____
_____
_____
_____
_____
_____
_____

COMPLETION DATE

_____

WOULD WE DO IT AGAIN?   YES ☐   NO ☐

OUR BUCKET LIST

WE WANT TO DO THIS BECAUSE

_____
_____
_____
_____

OUR MEMORIES AND THOUGHTS

_____
_____
_____
_____
_____
_____
_____
_____

COMPLETION DATE

_____

WOULD WE DO IT AGAIN?   YES ☐   NO ☐

OUR BUCKET LIST

WE WANT TO DO THIS BECAUSE

_____
_____
_____
_____

OUR MEMORIES AND THOUGHTS

_____
_____
_____
_____
_____
_____
_____
_____

COMPLETION DATE

_____

WOULD WE DO IT AGAIN?   YES ☐   NO ☐

OUR BUCKET LIST

WE WANT TO DO THIS BECAUSE

_____
_____
_____
_____
_____

OUR MEMORIES AND THOUGHTS

_____
_____
_____
_____
_____
_____
_____
_____
_____
_____

COMPLETION DATE

_____

WOULD WE DO IT AGAIN?   YES ☐   NO ☐

OUR BUCKET LIST

WE WANT TO DO THIS BECAUSE

_____
_____
_____
_____

OUR MEMORIES AND THOUGHTS

_____
_____
_____
_____
_____
_____
_____
_____
_____

COMPLETION DATE

_____

WOULD WE DO IT AGAIN?   YES ☐   NO ☐

OUR BUCKET LIST

WE WANT TO DO THIS BECAUSE

_____
_____
_____
_____

OUR MEMORIES AND THOUGHTS

_____
_____
_____
_____
_____
_____
_____
_____

COMPLETION DATE

_____

WOULD WE DO IT AGAIN?   YES ☐   NO ☐

OUR BUCKET LIST

WE WANT TO DO THIS BECAUSE

_____
_____
_____
_____

OUR MEMORIES AND THOUGHTS

_____
_____
_____
_____
_____
_____
_____
_____

COMPLETION DATE

_____

WOULD WE DO IT AGAIN?   YES ☐   NO ☐

OUR BUCKET LIST

WE WANT TO DO THIS BECAUSE

_____
_____
_____
_____

OUR MEMORIES AND THOUGHTS

_____
_____
_____
_____
_____
_____
_____
_____

COMPLETION DATE

_____

WOULD WE DO IT AGAIN?   YES ☐   NO ☐

OUR BUCKET LIST

WE WANT TO DO THIS BECAUSE

_____
_____
_____
_____

OUR MEMORIES AND THOUGHTS

_____
_____
_____
_____
_____
_____
_____
_____

COMPLETION DATE

_____

WOULD WE DO IT AGAIN?   YES ☐   NO ☐

OUR BUCKET LIST

WE WANT TO DO THIS BECAUSE

_____
_____
_____
_____
_____

OUR MEMORIES AND THOUGHTS

_____
_____
_____
_____
_____
_____
_____
_____
_____

COMPLETION DATE

_____

WOULD WE DO IT AGAIN?   YES ☐   NO ☐

OUR BUCKET LIST

WE WANT TO DO THIS BECAUSE

_____
_____
_____
_____

OUR MEMORIES AND THOUGHTS

_____
_____
_____
_____
_____
_____
_____
_____

COMPLETION DATE

_____

WOULD WE DO IT AGAIN?   YES ☐   NO ☐

OUR BUCKET LIST

WE WANT TO DO THIS BECAUSE

_____
_____
_____
_____

OUR MEMORIES AND THOUGHTS

_____
_____
_____
_____
_____
_____
_____
_____

COMPLETION DATE

_____

WOULD WE DO IT AGAIN?   YES ☐   NO ☐

OUR BUCKET LIST

WE WANT TO DO THIS BECAUSE

_____
_____
_____
_____

OUR MEMORIES AND THOUGHTS

_____
_____
_____
_____
_____
_____
_____
_____

COMPLETION DATE

_____

WOULD WE DO IT AGAIN?   YES ☐   NO ☐

OUR BUCKET LIST

WE WANT TO DO THIS BECAUSE

_____
_____
_____
_____

OUR MEMORIES AND THOUGHTS

_____
_____
_____
_____
_____
_____
_____
_____

COMPLETION DATE

_____

WOULD WE DO IT AGAIN?   YES ☐   NO ☐

OUR BUCKET LIST

WE WANT TO DO THIS BECAUSE

_____
_____
_____
_____

OUR MEMORIES AND THOUGHTS

_____
_____
_____
_____
_____
_____
_____
_____

COMPLETION DATE

_____

WOULD WE DO IT AGAIN?   YES ☐   NO ☐

OUR BUCKET LIST

WE WANT TO DO THIS BECAUSE

_____
_____
_____
_____
_____

OUR MEMORIES AND THOUGHTS

_____
_____
_____
_____
_____
_____
_____
_____
_____

COMPLETION DATE

_____

WOULD WE DO IT AGAIN?   YES ☐   NO ☐

OUR BUCKET LIST

WE WANT TO DO THIS BECAUSE

_____
_____
_____
_____

OUR MEMORIES AND THOUGHTS

_____
_____
_____
_____
_____
_____
_____
_____

COMPLETION DATE

_____

WOULD WE DO IT AGAIN?　　YES ☐　　NO ☐

OUR BUCKET LIST

WE WANT TO DO THIS BECAUSE

_____
_____
_____
_____

OUR MEMORIES AND THOUGHTS

_____
_____
_____
_____
_____
_____
_____
_____

COMPLETION DATE

_____

WOULD WE DO IT AGAIN?   YES ☐   NO ☐

OUR BUCKET LIST

WE WANT TO DO THIS BECAUSE

_____
_____
_____
_____

OUR MEMORIES AND THOUGHTS

_____
_____
_____
_____
_____
_____
_____
_____

COMPLETION DATE

_____

WOULD WE DO IT AGAIN?   YES ☐   NO ☐

OUR BUCKET LIST

WE WANT TO DO THIS BECAUSE

_____
_____
_____
_____
_____

OUR MEMORIES AND THOUGHTS

_____
_____
_____
_____
_____
_____
_____
_____

COMPLETION DATE

_____

WOULD WE DO IT AGAIN?　　YES ☐　　NO ☐

OUR BUCKET LIST

WE WANT TO DO THIS BECAUSE

_____
_____
_____
_____

OUR MEMORIES AND THOUGHTS

_____
_____
_____
_____
_____
_____
_____
_____

COMPLETION DATE

_____

WOULD WE DO IT AGAIN?   YES ☐   NO ☐

OUR BUCKET LIST

WE WANT TO DO THIS BECAUSE

_____
_____
_____
_____
_____

OUR MEMORIES AND THOUGHTS

_____
_____
_____
_____
_____
_____
_____
_____
_____
_____

COMPLETION DATE

_____

WOULD WE DO IT AGAIN?   YES ☐   NO ☐

OUR BUCKET LIST

WE WANT TO DO THIS BECAUSE

_____
_____
_____
_____

OUR MEMORIES AND THOUGHTS

_____
_____
_____
_____
_____
_____
_____
_____

COMPLETION DATE

_____

WOULD WE DO IT AGAIN?   YES ☐   NO ☐

OUR BUCKET LIST

WE WANT TO DO THIS BECAUSE

_____
_____
_____
_____

OUR MEMORIES AND THOUGHTS

_____
_____
_____
_____
_____
_____
_____
_____

COMPLETION DATE

_____

WOULD WE DO IT AGAIN?   YES ☐   NO ☐

OUR BUCKET LIST

WE WANT TO DO THIS BECAUSE

_____
_____
_____
_____

OUR MEMORIES AND THOUGHTS

_____
_____
_____
_____
_____
_____
_____
_____

COMPLETION DATE

_____

WOULD WE DO IT AGAIN?   YES ☐   NO ☐

www.ingramcontent.com/pod-product-compliance
Lightning Source LLC
LaVergne TN
LVHW011957070526
838202LV00054B/4949